CONTENTS

STATEMENTS

APPENDIX

PREPARED STATEMENTS

THE FUTURE OF DEMOCRACY IN HONG KONG

THURSDAY, NOVEMBER 20, 2014

CONGRESSIONAL-EXECUTIVE
COMMISSION ON CHINA,
Washington, DC.

The hearing was convened, pursuant to notice, at 3:46 p.m., in Room G–50, Dirksen Senate Office Building, Hon. Sherrod Brown, Chairman, presiding.

Also Present: Representatives Christopher Smith, Cochairman and Robert Pittenger and Senator Ben Cardin.

OPENING STATEMENT OF HON. SHERROD BROWN, A U.S. SENATOR FROM OHIO; CHAIRMAN, CONGRESSIONAL–EXECUTIVE COMMISSION ON CHINA

Chairman BROWN. The commission will come to order. I thank the second panel for being here and thanks for your patience to start a moment late. We had votes on the Senate floor and thank you for your willingness to wait for the first 45 more minutes or so for Lord Patten to do his remarks and take questions.

So thank you for your cooperation and always thanks to Congressman Smith who has just been terrific working with on this Commission, whether he is Chair and I am Vice Chair or I am Chair and he is Vice Chair.

We recently introduced legislation, Congressman Smith and I, to renew our commitment to freedom and democracy in Hong Kong. It is the first time that we figure, going back in the history of this Commission, that the two cochairs—always of separate Houses, opposite parties—have come forward and introduced legislation jointly. It speaks to the seriousness of this issue. It speaks to the consensus if not unanimity of both parties in both Houses of Congress in the importance of this, the rightness of this and the concern we all have about what has happened in Hong Kong.

The People's Republic of China made a promise to the international community and to the people of Hong Kong that they would enjoy certain freedoms and could freely elect their leaders. It is those freedoms and autonomy that have ensured Hong Kong's—in many ways—miraculous stability and prosperity.

But now the People's Republic of China is backtracking on these promises, not only that, some in China are seeking to distract from this issue by claiming that the United States is behind these protests. No straight right-thinking person really believes that, although that continues to be put out in some quarters, apparently, of the Chinese Government.

(1)

The desire of the people of Hong Kong for freedom and for democracy is genuine. By holding this hearing, we urge China to respect their calls for democracy and to make good on its promise.

Lord Patten will speak about that promise, will speak about the Basic Law, will speak about what he saw and what he heard and what he was promised almost two decades ago in the years leading up to 1997. Only by doing so, by holding this hearing, by China respecting their calls for democracy and making good on its promise, only by doing so can we have faith in China's commitment to international law.

I look forward to the testimony of Lord Patten and our other three witnesses whom I will introduce at the appropriate time and I call on Congressman Smith.

STATEMENT OF HON. CHRISTOPHER SMITH, A U.S. REPRESENTATIVE FROM NEW JERSEY; COCHAIRMAN, CONGRESSIONAL–EXECUTIVE COMMISSION ON CHINA

Representative SMITH. Thank you very much, Chairman Brown. It is a real honor to work with you not only on the Commission but on our new Hong Kong legislation which has now been jointly introduced and we will stay with that until it becomes law. So thank you for that leadership and for that cooperation of working side-by-side.

Democrat or Republican, we care about the people of Hong Kong. We care about human rights and this is another manifestation of that kind of bipartisanship.

I would like to welcome our witnesses, as well, to this important gathering, this hearing to testify. I look out and see Mark Lagon who was our distinguished Ambassador working to combat human trafficking. He did a superb job in that position and has really made a difference and left a legacy and a lasting mark.

I want to welcome our other witnesses too. They have just done tremendous things for so long. I also welcome Lord Patten.

I remember visiting Lord Patten when I visited High Island during the Comprehensive Agreement with regard to boat people. He received my delegation and was extremely hospitable and as always knowledgeable.

He also testified at a hearing on human rights that I held years ago on the Patten Commission Recommendations to help really to open up transparent policing in northern Ireland. Those Commission recommendations that he headed has had a lasting effect on good proper policing in the north of Ireland.

This is the second public event that the Commission has held on the issue of Hong Kong. In April, the Commission heard from Martin Lee and Anson Chan, two leaders of Hong Kong's political world.

Their work, as well as the work of Hong Kong's new generation of leaders has inspired this Commission and the U.S. Congress and freedom-loving people throughout the world. As has been mentioned already, Senator Brown and I have introduced bills in the House and Senate to update U.S. policy on Hong Kong. I've also agreed to start a Congressional Hong Kong caucus on the House side to demonstrate that Congress is concerned about Hong Kong's

autonomy and its importance to U.S. national interests as well as global interests.

As our witnesses today will attest, under the "one country, two systems" model, China guaranteed that Hong Kong would retain its separate political, legal, and economic systems for at least 50 years. Hong Kong's Constitution, the Basic Law, protects the rights of the people of Hong Kong to free speech, assembly, and the power to choose their own government, ultimately through universal suffrage.

These promises were made to the people of Hong Kong and to the international community. Instead of keeping these promises, Beijing has decided to stack the deck against democracy and the rule of law, demanding that both judges and any future Chief Executive must "love the country and love Hong Kong."

But, in August of this year, they ruled that the people of Hong Kong could not freely choose their next leader. Such demands will undermine an independent judiciary and make the 2017 Chief Executive election look more like an Iranian election then one that is free and fair.

The slow erosion of press freedoms and the rule of law, the setbacks to Hong Kong's democratic developments, and Beijing's less than subtle oversight of Hong Kong are the reasons the protests materialized and why they are ongoing. No matter what is said by President Xi Jinping or other Chinese officials, the "Umbrella Movement" was a creation of Beijing's policies and its rough oversight.

There is no "Black Hand" of foreign forces behind the protests, only requests for Beijing to live up to its promises and to ensure Hong Kong's unique system of autonomy within China. Hong Kong's unique system has ensured prosperity and spurred the type of creativity that only comes with the advance of fundamental freedoms. The freedoms of speech, assembly, association, and religion, and an independent judiciary, are the foundation on which Hong Kong's continued prosperity and stability are based.

That is what the people of Hong Kong want. It is what they have conveyed to their leaders and to Beijing repeatedly for the last 17 years. Hong Kong's continued autonomy and the advance of its democracy is a deep concern of the U.S. Congress and freedom-loving people all over the world.

I thank my friend for calling this important hearing. I yield back.

Chairman BROWN. Thank you Chairman Smith.

Mr. Pittenger, welcome.

STATEMENT OF HON. ROBERT PITTENGER, A U.S. REPRESENTATIVE FROM NORTH CAROLINA

Representative PITTENGER. Thank you, Chairman Brown and thank you, Chairman Smith, particularly, for your leadership on behalf of freedom-loving people around the world and for the human rights and dignity of all people.

And thank you to the witnesses who are appearing before us today to discuss such an important movement. The First Amendment of the U.S. Constitution affords American citizens the rights to freedom of speech, freedom of the press, and freedom to peace-

fully assemble. These rights are the foundation of our democracy. These rights are what have allowed America to continually grow and to advance. They are what continue to make America a beacon of freedom to the world.

America, however, must continue to advocate for these rights to be afforded to every person around the world. I would say to you today that the independent courageous members of the ''Umbrella Movement,'' they are seeking to bring a true democracy to Hong Kong. China now has the opportunity to ensure that the intent of ''one country, two systems'' is being upheld as promised.

America must be clear in our support for Hong Kong and the ideals of liberty and democracy. I look forward to hearing from our witnesses about how the events in Hong Kong have brought us to our current state and what role America can play to help ensure that they do achieve a true democracy.

Thank you, Mr. Chairman and I yield back.

Chairman BROWN. Thank you Congressman Pittenger and thank you for your involvement and regular input into this Commission.

Representative PITTENGER. It is my honor.

Chairman BROWN. Lord Patten, welcome. Thank you so much for joining us. The Honorable Lord Patten of Barnes served as the last British Governor of Hong Kong from 1992 to 1997. He oversaw the last years of British rule and Hong Kong's reversion to Chinese sovereignty.

After his time as Governor, Lord Patten was European Commissioner for External Affairs for five years, Chairman of the BBC Trust for three more years. He currently serves as the Chancellor of Oxford University. He is testifying today via video link from London.

Lord Patten, if you would begin your five-minute opening statement. Again, thank you for your patience. Thank you for giving us an hour today and your public service.

Lord Patten?

STATEMENT OF RT. HON. LORD PATTEN OF BARNES CH: 28TH GOVERNOR OF HONG KONG, 1992–1997; CHANCELLOR UNIVERSITY OF OXFORD (Appearing live via video teleconference)

Lord PATTEN. First of all thank you very much indeed for inviting me and I will be as brief as possible because in the limited time we have, I would like to give you the maximum opportunity to ask questions and to invigilate, I hope, my responses.

I do at the outset want to pick up a point that you've made already and then to add a little to it. You mentioned that there is a constant barrage of criticism from Beijing and indeed from some in Hong Kong that this democratic movement, the pressure for and sustaining the rule of law, democracy pluralism in Hong Kong is all organized from outside. And it is suggested that any interest taken by people outside is an unfair interference in China's own business.

I think there are three very obvious responses to that. First of all, the Joint Declaration which was the basis for the transfer of sovereignty from the United Kingdom to China, the Joint Declaration is a treaty between China and Britain. The main beneficiaries

of the treaty are the people of Hong Kong, but there are obligations under the treaty.

There were obligations which Britain had to China before 1997 and since 1997 which China has to Britain. And it is absurd to argue that we shouldn't talk about the Joint Declaration. It is not a Chinese declaration, it is a Joint Declaration.

Second, China should recognize that Hong Kong is a great international city. There are, I think, 1,200 American businesses there, just to take one example. There is a large American community and it is in America's and everyone's interest that Hong Kong should continue to be a bastion of enterprise and rule of law in Asia with all of the freedoms that we associate with a liberal and plural society.

I think it is perfectly natural and indeed to be welcomed that consistently the Congress, Senate, House of Representatives have shown an interest in what is happening in Hong Kong. When I was governor there, the American Chamber of Commerce were extremely supportive as were the State Department when we tried to make the best of the arrangements for elections to ensure that they were as democratic as possible.

Third, it is quite interesting that in the last couple of days the Russian Deputy Defense Minister in discussions with his Chinese opposite number has been suggesting that perhaps the Russians can help China deal with their problems in Hong Kong, that this is like what happened in the Ukraine. I haven't heard Chinese Foreign Ministry spokesmen or others in China saying it is disgraceful that the Russians should be interfering in the affairs of Hong Kong.

It is a slur on the wonderfully principled young people in Hong Kong and others—not those who in the last few days, a very small minority, who have protested violently, but all of those others who have been involved in this movement.

It is a slur on them to pretend that they are somehow puppets of outsiders. It is a disgrace to suggest that and I think they have behaved admirably.

The other thing I want to say is that, what they have been doing is, of course, refusing to accept that they can have their future stolen. They have been trying to argue that one of the best ways of sustaining the rule of law and all of the freedoms that we would associate with a liberal society is by having the ability to elect their own leaders, to elect their own government.

I think it is extremely sad that the government in Hong Kong hasn't shown any statesmanship in trying to move toward a dialogue with the students and find ways in which they can give the students a way of—at least at the present stage of their campaign—reaching a short-term agreement about how to take things forward. There were all sorts of things that could've been suggested since last July.

I have written about several of them, both related to the next Legislative Council elections in 2016 and to the election of the Chief Executive in 2017. There are lots of things which would've been absolutely within the gift of the Hong Kong authorities to have done and they haven't done any of them.

Finally, I am sure that the Chinese authorities understand that there are responsibilities which come with a growing economic and political power in the world. I think there is now a gulf between the economic authority of China—though, I know some people are concerned about what happens next to the Chinese economy—and the lack of, as it were, soft power in China and I think that is affected by the way it behaves over Hong Kong and there were other similar issues.

So I think this is a big and defining issue for how China is going to behave in the 21st century. I have absolutely no doubt at all that Joshua Wong and the other students who have been supporting him with this exemplary example of how to demonstrate for principles—I think that Joshua Wong and his colleagues own the future and I don't think it is owned by those whose view apparently is that the problem about allowing people elections, is you don't know the results in advance and the problem about allowing people elections is that as the Chief Executive in Hong Kong suggested, if everybody can vote, you will have lots of people who have below median incomes who can vote and what on Earth will happen as he seems to suggest—when poor people can vote as well. Well, I suppose that is socialism with Chinese characteristics, but it is not my idea of how to build a plural society.

Chairman BROWN. Thank you very much, Lord Patten, for your insight. We are joined today by Senator Cardin who is not a member of this Commission, but is perhaps the most learned and outspoken advocate for human rights in the entire U.S. Senate, so Senator Cardin, thank you for joining us.

Let me start. Lord Patten has until 4 o'clock our time and we obviously want to take advantage of his time and to respect his time.

Lord Patten, when you prepared, you and the British Government, the Hong Kong Government prepared for the handover in 1997, what impression were you given by Chinese officials about their willingness to allow Hong Kong to be democratic, and were the British confident that Hong Kong would be allowed to have democratic elections of their Chief Executive and of their Legislative Council?

Lord PATTEN. While there are two particular documents which—and I don't want to sound too much like a lawyer, I am married to one, but I am not one. There are two particular documents that I should refer to.

The first is the Joint Declaration which was the treaty between Britain and China lodged at the United Nations which determined the handover. The Joint Declaration talks about the freedoms of Hong Kong, about the rule of law. It talks about the legislature holding the executive to account. It talks about the leader of the executive being elected. But it doesn't specify electoral arrangements.

Then after the Joint Declaration, there was the Chinese Basic Law which was the mini constitution for Hong Kong. It is the Basic Law which is supposed to implement the principles of the Joint Declaration—''one country, two systems''—and to spell out the actual electoral arrangements. To be honest, the electoral arrangements were, to some extent after 1997, a bit vague.

They were quite explicit before 1997 and what I tried to do when I was Governor from 1992 to 1997 was to make the arrangements we had agreed with the Chinese as open and democratic as possible. I did not go beyond the terms of the Basic Law, but I increased the number of people able to vote by about 2.7 million.

I think what I did was inevitably limited by the agreements that had already been made and I was surprised to be both lionized for being a great democratic champion and vilified for what I was doing. I think I was doing pretty much the minimum of what was required in order to ensure that the elections were as fair and reasonable as possible.

I have said in the past, I have written in the past, that I don't think in the years before that we had done as much as we should've done to entrench democracy. That was of course partly, as the documents now suggest, the documents which have been opened, because the Chinese were very much against us moving to greater democracy in Hong Kong because they thought it might lead people in Hong Kong to think they were eventually going to be independent like, say Singapore, or other places where we had been the colonial power.

So it is complete nonsense to suggest that China always wanted democracy in Hong Kong. It was very resistant to any form of democracy in Hong Kong.

When we left in 1997, I thought two things. First of all, I was pretty sure that the Chinese would roll back the rather limited increase in the electorate that I had made, but I did think that the Chinese would keep their word under the Basic Law and that democracy would inevitably develop.

Margaret Thatcher who was the Prime Minister who negotiated the Joint Declaration said in our Parliament, and the House that I am in now and where I have to go in order to speak and vote a little later—so I apologize for that—she said in 1992, in December, that she hoped that there would be a fully democratically elected legislature by 2007. Now that wasn't an explicit promise made by the Chinese, but we were certainly promised that we would be on the road to democracy.

Perhaps I can read out one particular passage from the Basic Law, from Article 45 about the Chief Executive. First of all it is clear under the Basic Law that the arrangements for the election of the legislature are for the Government of Hong Kong—for the Government of Hong Kong to report to Beijing, but not to get the authority or agreement of Beijing for those arrangements. So there is plenty that the Government of Hong Kong could be doing on that front.

As far as the Chief Executive is concerned, Article 45 of the Basic Law says this: ''The method for selecting the Chief Executive shall be specified in the light of the actual situation in the Hong Kong Special Administrative Region and in accordance with the principle of gradual and orderly progress. The ultimate aim is the selection of the Chief Executive by universal suffrage upon nomination by a broadly representative nominating committee in accordance with democratic procedures.''

Now, the actual situation in the Hong Kong Special Administrative Region is one in which there are huge numbers of people argu-

ing for a proper democratic election, a proper democratic procedure to choose the Chief Executive. The principle of gradual and orderly progress. This is 2014.

It is 17 years since I sailed away from Hong Kong, plenty of time to run a gradual and orderly progress toward democracy. The ultimate aim is the selection of the Chief Executive by universal suffrage upon nomination by a broadly representative nominating committee. The nominating committee represents 7.5 percent of the electorate.

So what you have been given at the end of this whole process is the sort of election, the sort of democratic election which would be understood in Iran where the leadership can decide who you are allowed to vote for. I think that it is those proposals which have provoked the present protests, the present demonstrations, the ''Umbrella Movement'' and I am extremely sorry that the leadership in Beijing and the leadership in Hong Kong haven't entered into a proper dialogue with the students.

I am very unhappy that they seem to believe that if they simply allow things to run on and on and on, sooner or later a few people on the fringes will behave in ways which the students themselves deplore and that has started to happen. But I really do think that you cannot solve this problem by simply putting it off.

You can't put the police in the position where they have to make up for the lack of sensible politics. There are plenty of ways in which there could be accommodations with the students which would ensure that elections were free and fair and provided the sort of outcome which the International Covenant on Civil and Political Rights [ICCPR] which was also put into the Hong Kong Constitution guarantees.

Chairman BROWN. Thank you Lord Patten.

Chairman Smith?

Representative SMITH. Thank you very much. Lord Patten, thank you for your testimony. Thank you for your leadership. You give us clear and insightful comments today.

Let me just ask you if I could and I thank you for your words about the slur on the integrity and principles of Hong Kong's citizens to assert that the Chinese Government's propaganda machine, as it does, that they are being manipulated by outside forces. That cannot be said often enough and without enough exclamation points because unaccustomed as they are, the Chinese Government always slurs and libels those who speak the truth and here is another serious manifestation of that. So thank you for bringing attention to that.

Let me ask you, under Hu Jintao and now under Xi Jinping, do you discern any difference in how they have approached Hong Kong or are the events now being driven in part by the calendar as 2017 approaches?

With regard to the rights, are you finding that some human rights are more at risk and are being violated more aggressively by the leadership in Hong Kong as well as in Beijing? And is it getting worse by the day, week or month?

And if you could just tell us how has the United Kingdom monitored China and Hong Kong's compliance with the joint declaration and since it was registered as a treaty with the United Na-

tions, how has the UN monitored China and Hong Kong's compliance with that important agreement?

Lord PATTEN. First of all, there is plenty of difference between Xi Jinping and Hu Jintao. I am not sure, with one exception, you can demonstrate it in what they have done about Hong Kong. Clearly Xi Jinping is a much more powerful leader than Hu Jintao. Deng Xiaoping, after the years of Mao, deemed it sensible to try to put in place after him a more consensual, a broader leadership. So with both Jiang Zemin and Hu Jintao, they had premiers and colleagues, and governed with those leaders. I think clearly Xi Jinping is a much more imperial leader.

I think there are three reasons for that. First of all, I think the leadership was spooked by the whole Bo Xilai affair. Second, I think there was a feeling that there had been drift during the Hu Jintao period, whether that is fair or not I would not say.

Third, I think Xi Jinping is clearly one hell of an operator and I think that given the chance, he has pushed others aside and assumed huge numbers of powers himself. Now, he clearly wants to reform the economy and particularly the balance between state-owned enterprises and the private sector.

I guess that one consideration he has is that if he is going to move in what some would regard as a rather moderate direction on the economy, he has to be tough on the politics. If you look at what has happened in China in the last year or so, there has been a really tough clampdown, crackdown on humans rights lawyers, on dissidents, and on the blogosphere, and on Chinese Twitter and anybody who has got out of line has been hit for six.

One example of that, I guess, is that those who have argued that senior leaders should declare their assets publicly which would be a very good way of meeting some of the President Xi Jinping's ambitions on dealing with corruption have been locked up. It is not the people who have those Rolex watches and tax havens overseas who have been, in every case, put in jail.

It has been argued that there should be greater openness. So there has been a crackdown on all of those political manifestations and it may be that Hong Kong has suffered as a result. I think there is also a sense in the leadership—though this is stabbing in the dark—I think there's also a sense that the leadership having backed down a few years ago over the attempt to introduce a law of subversion in Hong Kong and the leadership having backed down when Joshua Wong and other students objected to changing the curriculum in order to introduce more ''Chinese Communist patriotism'' into it, that they wouldn't back down for a third time. So I think it may be caught up in that whole issue of politics in Beijing, but it is obviously very difficult to say.

On the rule of law, there was a Chinese white paper which was produced earlier this year and it encouraged me, for the first time, to speak out in Hong Kong. I had written about Hong Kong, but on the whole, while I have gone back to Hong Kong and I've been really pleased to do so, I haven't spoken about Hong Kong with great regularity because I thought that was slightly unseemly.

But I did speak out this year when a white paper was produced in Beijing which, to many people, seemed to be undermining the rule of law. It was a point made by a large number of barristers

who demonstrated—I think 1,700 of them demonstrated—in front of the Court of Final Appeal, the Bar Association objected; the Law Society President had to resign because he seemed to have defended the Chinese position.

And the former Chief Justice of Hong Kong spoke out suggesting that any implication that Hong Kong judges should be patriotic in the way that the Chinese Communist Party was suggesting would undermine their judicial independence. So that was an unsettling moment for the rule of law in Hong Kong.

And of course we know that the Chinese leadership have some difficulty in understanding the rule of law. I think they believe in rule by law, but ruled by the law that the party puts in place rather than rule of law.

Now you asked about the United Kingdom Government and I know that there is a tradition in American politics that you don't rubbish your own government when you are overseas and I would not want to be too critical of my own government in these hearings which I much welcome.

Representative SMITH. Lord Patten, if I could interrupt? It was just to ask you whether or not there is compliance——

Lord PATTEN. If I could be very diplomatic, I would say that I think that the British Government has been restrained in its comments on what has been happening in Hong Kong. It produces a six-monthly report on the affairs in Hong Kong and that is a fairly neutral and—I've said myself—rather anodyne document.

The Prime Minister has called for people to be given a genuine choice in Hong Kong and he has also spoken out in favor of the right of people to demonstrate under the rule of law in Hong Kong. That is all welcomed. But I hope that British Ministers will note what the American Government has said about Hong Kong, what President Obama said during the APEC [Asia-Pacific Economic Cooperation] meetings recently and I think that should be extremely welcome.

You will, I am sure, know or want to know that a body which is similar to your own in the United Kingdom Parliament, the Foreign Affairs Committee of the House of Commons, is at present undertaking hearings on Hong Kong. They have been talking about going to Hong Kong to take evidence themselves. And their interest in Hong Kong has been denounced, as you would expect, by the Chinese authorities who regarded it as a monstrous interference.

But as I said earlier, we have a treaty with China and as I also said earlier, I haven't heard any Chinese authorities denouncing the Russian Defense Minister for what he said recently about helping in Hong Kong.

Chairman BROWN. Thank you Lord Patten.

Congressman Pittenger?

Representative PITTENGER. Thank you, Mr. Chairman. Lord Patten, how would you counsel the "Umbrella Movement" today as they move forward and then also my second part is how would you counsel America and its role? I had one American businessman in Hong Kong tell me that our engagement, our involvement could be counterproductive. It could be seen as America is being the one who is behind this movement. I would really appreciate your good insight in these two questions.

And I would also appreciate that response from the rest of our friends who have come on the panel today. Thank you very much.

Lord PATTEN. Can I say a word, first of all, about the U.S. engagement? I say it in this context. I don't believe it is in any of our interests in the years ahead for China to do badly. You can't possibly want 1.3 billion people to do badly and it would be the worst threat to the global economy or to us politically for China to come a cropper, for China to do badly.

So I hope China thrives and prospers and I think it is more likely to thrive and prosper sustainably if it enjoys political change and greater accountability and not just economic change. I think economic and political freedom are closely integrated.

So to come to the specific point about U.S. engagement, there is a very quaint notion that you can never disagree with China, that whatever China does, it is the Middle Kingdom and you have to go along with it and that if you don't go along with it, you risk not being able to sell things to China, you risk doing damage to your economy.

I think I am right in saying that China's exports to the United States went up by 1,600 percent in 15 years. So who needs whom?

We live—it is cliché—in an interdependent world. I think it is ridiculous to suggest that any attempt to stand up for our values or for what we believe in means risking economic damage in our relationship with China.

I think the reason why China buys products from America or Germany or Britain—not so many from Britain—is because it wants those things at the best price it can buy them for. I think it is, in a way, encouraging China to behave badly, to continually suggest that it is only if we ignore them behaving badly that we can continue with a satisfactory economic relationship. I really do think it has been a besetting sin of our relationship with China over the years.

If I may enter into an American political debate for a moment, I don't think that the United States or anybody else reacting critically when China does things that we disagree with is tantamount to containing China or confronting China or launching an Asian Cold War with China. I think we would behave with China as we should behave with other countries and try to develop a relationship based on principle and on our national interests.

Representative PITTENGER. Lord Patten, If I could ask you——

Lord PATTEN [continuing]. I think the relationship between China and the United States will be fundamental to the sort of century we live in and the peace and prosperity of this century. There is a sort of "smart Alec" point which some historians argue about suggesting that China and America relations risk dumping us in what they call the "Thucydides trap." The suggestion is that inevitably a rising power always fetches up in a violent confrontation with the existing superpower as happened with Sparta and Athens in the 5th century B.C., with Germany in the 19th century, but I don't believe that is true at all.

The advice I would give to students, and I would be hesitant in the area of doing so because I think they behaved with such extraordinary principle and good sense themselves and I am sad that their efforts in the last couple of days have been besmirched by the

activities of the few rowdies, I think what I would say to them is this: You have won the argument and Hong Kong and you have won the argument because you've continued to stand on the moral high ground. You have continued doing that and you are now behaving in a way which recognizes the rule of law. So that however dignified, however important your cause, if there are court injunctions to move out of a particular area, they have to be obeyed. The students have been doing that.

I think it would say to them the government is not helping you by behaving as it should in a statesmanlike way, but everybody recognizes that. Everybody recognizes that the government hasn't even done the bare minimum to provide you with some way in which there could be an accommodation.

But it doesn't mean you have lost. This is a campaign that can be continued and will be continued in other ways. So I think I would for the time being, at least, drop down a few notches with this campaign but be prepared to continue it in other ways in the future.

I have really been impressed by these kids standing up for the sort of things we take for granted—bravely, decently. If they were my kids I would be really proud of them.

Chairman BROWN. Thank you and in respect to your time, Lord Patten, I have one brief question. If you could be a bit prescriptive, how do the United States and the United Kingdom best work together to support Hong Kong's democracy in light of your answer if you would kind of continue that to Congressman Pittenger, what points of leverage do our two countries and others have to pressure China to fulfill these international commitments? If you would give us sort of the last five minutes and then in respect to your time, we will let you out by I believe 9 o'clock your time. Thank you.

Lord PATTEN. [Inaudible.] Thank you very much. Indeed we have them here as well.

Look, I think the very fact that you are holding these hearings, the very fact that you are talking about continuing without being interfering but continuing because of the principles which underpin your work to take a regular interest in what is happening in Hong Kong, I think that matters hugely. I think the fact that the Foreign Affairs Select Committee of the House of Commons here is conducting hearings like this despite assaults on its integrity by the Chinese Embassy here, by Chinese officials. I think that helps.

I think having a focus on what is happening in Hong Kong is enormously important. There is a comparison I would like to draw, if I may, which you may think is a little far-fetched, but I think it really does apply.

In the days of the Soviet Union, when the Soviet Union was locking up dissidents—Mr. Putin is still locking up dissidents. When they were locking up dissidents then, we used to say to dissidents sometimes when they were let out, "Was it a help or was it a hindrance when Western countries raised your case?"

Some people would always say then "Oh, it is always better if you talk about this in private. If you talk about it in public, if you make a fuss about it, the authorities will be much tougher."

The dissidents themselves would always say it made a difference when you raised their cases publicly, when you raised the ante for

the authorities. I think it is exactly the same with dissidents in China. I think it is exactly the same with those who are arguing for democracy in Hong Kong.

I am quite surprised, I have to say, that we don't raise the questions about dissidents as much as we used to or about religious freedom as much as we used to, when we talk to Chinese officials. I think we should do it more. But I certainly think that by talking about the importance of Hong Kong continuing to have its autonomy, continuing to have its freedoms and having those freedoms underpinned by democratic development, I think simply talking about that, I think shining a spotlight on that really does matter. I think it matters to China and I think if it didn't matter to China, the Chinese wouldn't make such a fuss when you hold hearings like this or when others hold hearings.

So I don't think that there is some recourse we can have to a United Nations trigger, though that is always suggested by people. It may be possible, but I don't have quite as much confidence in the ability to take that route as some others have. I think actually talking about these issues, I think making a public case about them matters enormously and for me, one of the important things in the last few weeks has been reading the constant and very accurate reports in American newspapers about what is happening in Hong Kong.

I think the television coverage by the BBC, as well, has been extremely good and I think all of those things matter hugely. They matter hugely to a country which is going to help shape our futures, China, but which doesn't have as much soft power around the world as you would think, which is why I guess its principal friends are apparently Venezuela, Zimbabwe, and North Korea.

Chairman BROWN. Lord Patten, thank you for sharing your evening. Good night. Enjoy the rest of your evening and we will enjoy the rest of our afternoon. Thank you.

Lord PATTEN. Thank you very much. It has been a privilege.

Chairman BROWN. Thank you. Ours too.

[Applause.]

Chairman BROWN. Let me introduce our panel and thank the three of you for joining us.

Professor Victoria Tin-bor Hui is assistant professor and political science faculty fellow at the Liu Institute for Asia and Asian Studies at the University of Notre Dame. Professor Hui's research includes Chinese political history and theories of the state as well as ''contentious policies and resistance movements.'' Since the beginning of the demonstrations in Hong Kong, Professor Hui has maintained a blog to explain the protest movement in the context of constitutionalism and human rights.

She grew up in Hong Kong. She recently visited Hong Kong to observe the protests. Welcome.

Ambassador Mark Lagon is currently the chair for global politics and security at Georgetown's Master of Science in Foreign Service Program and adjunct senior fellow for human rights on the Council for Foreign Relations. From 2007 to 2009, he served as U.S. Ambassador-At-Large directing the Office to Monitor and Combat Trafficking in Persons.

In January 2015, he will become president of the Freedom House. Welcome, Ambassador.

Dr. Richard Bush—good to see you again—is a senior fellow at Brookings, director of the Center for East Asian Policy Study. He holds the Chen-Fu and Cecilia Yen Koo Chair in Taiwan Studies.

Doctor Bush worked on the staff of the House Foreign Affairs Committee from 1983 to 1995. When I first met him, he was the chairman and managing director of the American Institute in Taiwan from 1997 to 2002. He is currently engaged in a study on the economic and political future of Hong Kong. Dr. Bush recently returned from Hong Kong where he, like Dr. Hui, observed the demonstrations.

We will begin with your testimony Dr. Hui. If you would keep it to approximately five minutes, each of you. Welcome.

STATEMENT OF VICTORIA TIN–BOR HUI, PH.D.: ASSOCIATE PROFESSOR, DEPARTMENT OF POLITICAL SCIENCE; FACULTY FELLOW, LIU INSTITUTE FOR ASIA AND ASIAN STUDIES, UNIVERSITY OF NOTRE DAME

Ms. HUI. Thank you so much for having me here. I'm very proud of my Hong Kong origin, but today I shall speak as an academic expert. Because I don't claim to speak for protesters who have faced down police forces and thug violence, I only wish to highlight the significance of what they have been doing.

The protesters' demands are best captured by this yellow banner that you can see everywhere in Hong Kong. ''We want genuine universalsuffrage.''

This refers to the right to nominate candidates as well as the right to vote for the next Chief Executive in 2017. The ''Umbrella Movement'' has witnessed hundreds of thousands of protesters occupying busy streets in Hong Kong. At the same time, the media has shown images of counter-protesters roughing up nonviolent protesters.

The division among Hong Kong people hinges on one question: Is it possible to preserve freedom without democracy? Hong Kong people, whether they are pro-occupy or anti-occupy, really desire freedom. They want a neutral civil service, an impartial police, an independent judiciary, and a free press. These core values are disappearing without democracy.

Hong Kong has seen three Chief Executives since 1997. They were chosen by a narrowly based election committee beholden to Beijing and so they have undercut Hong Kong's core values.

The first Chief Executive, C. H. Tung, under Beijing's prodding, introduced a draconian national security bill in 2003. He was forced to shelve the bill and then resign after a half-million protesters took to the streets. Now, these days, pro-establishment figures are talking about re-tabling the bill so as to stifle dissent in the future.

And then the second Chief Executive, Donald Tsang, introduced political appointments to top civil service positions without electoral accountability. This practice created cronyism and eroded the meritocratic civil service.

The third and current Chief Executive, CY Leung, has stepped up the appointments of his loyal supporters to key government po-

sitions and also advisory committees. This has further corrupted the government. Under his watch, even the Independent Commission Against Corruption, ICAC, has become the target of a corruption investigation. And worse, CY Leung has been accused of receiving payouts of HK$50 million and then $37 million from the Australian firm UGL without publicly reporting them.

In addition, the police have come under attack for making arbitrary arrests and selectively enforcing the law. Media critics of the government have been demoted or fired with some journalists being physically attacked by thugs.

So the rapid erosion of freedom has seriously undercut Hong Kong's promised autonomy. Protesters want genuine universal suffrage because the previous system of freedom without democracy is broken.

Some Hong Kong people, many in my generation and older, still believe that Hong Kong can keep its freedom without democracy. But this view actually goes against world trends. It is not coincidental that Hong Kong has been the only case of freedom without democracy in the world and this unique system is fast disappearing.

All around the world, freedom and democracy are either present together or absent together, strong together or weak together. It is simply impossible to preserve a meritocratic civil service, an impartial police, an independent judiciary, and a free press without democracy.

Now the protesters are loud and clear about the goal of universal franchise. It is not easy to get there. The ''Umbrella Movement'' is nearing the end of a second month. As the government has refused to have a meaningful dialogue with protesters, supporters are looking for alternative ways to sustain the movement beyond occupying busy streets.

I think it may be less daunting, although by no means easy, to put pressure on business elites who are in the position to influence the government. All over the world, business elites are naturally pro-regime, but they may have second thoughts if protesters can impose cost on the continued collusion with the government.

Protesters are circulating a list of businesses for a targeted boycott. The government plans to turn the 1,200-member election committee into a nominating committee for the chief executive in 2017. Leading members of this committee are Hong Kong's wealthiest tycoons who dominate most businesses and make money off every ordinary Hong Kong person.

Hong Kong's rich and famous may be convinced that keeping the economy open to the world depends on guarding Hong Kong's freedom with democracy. Their long-term interests are better served in a Hong Kong that remains an international city rather than a Hong Kong that becomes just another Chinese city.

Ultimately it is incumbent upon the Hong Kong Government to address protesters' demands. As bailiffs are clearing streets this week, the government may be tempted to think that the problem will simply go away. But the source of the problem is not the occupied movement. It is the government's erosion of freedom.

Protesters will continue to struggle with other forms of civil disobedience. And now that the government has also trained a fear-

less generation, repression can only backfire and is not an option. The government has no alternative but to reopen negotiations with the students on future electoral arrangements.

Hong Kong students say that history has chosen them. I think these students have shouldered this burden with immense courage. History has actually also chosen Hong Kong's powerful adults. It is their turn to make right choices. Thank you.

Chairman BROWN. Thank you Dr. Hui.

Ambassador Lagon?

STATEMENT OF AMBASSADOR MARK P. LAGON, PH.D.: GLOBAL POLITICS AND SECURITY CHAIR, MASTER OF SCIENCE IN FOREIGN SERVICE PROGRAM, GEORGETOWN, UNIVERSITY; ADJUNCT SENIOR FELLOW FOR HUMAN RIGHTS COUNCIL ON FOREIGN RELATIONS; INCOMING PRESIDENT, FREEDOM HOUSE

Ambassador LAGON. Thank you very much Chairman Brown, Cochairman Smith, and distinguished members of the Commission. It is really an honor to appear here today.

Optimists have hoped that because of Hong Kong's economic importance, China would honor its commitment to ''one country, two systems'' until 2047. Other optimists have hoped for Chinese leaders to usher in political reforms, but events in Hong Kong have provided evidence, unfortunately, to the contrary.

Hong Kong police, just a few weeks ago, aggressively deployed tear gas and arrested protesters, violating the right of peaceable assembly long protected under Article 27 of the Basic Law. Many were arrested, including the iconic student leader Joshua Wong, who was detained for nearly 40 hours before use of a habeas corpus petition—a petition China does not permit in the rest of the mainland.

What do events signal for human rights in Hong Kong? Will we see a continued push by China to assume ultimate control of Hong Kong? Freedoms in Hong Kong have declined since the handover. Press freedom—Freedom House has found—is at its lowest point in a decade. Beijing has attempted to introduce a propagandistic curriculum in Hong Kong schools, and the white paper released by Beijing stating that all city administrators and—notably—judges must love China are very troubling.

The 1,200-member nominating committee vetting candidates for the next Chief Executive will be based on the current election committee comprised of special interests and weighted heavily toward pro-CCP [Chinese Communist Party] members.

Second, despite any polls taken this week, there is strong popular support for democracy and human rights. A history of rights-based law has enabled Hong Kong to become an economic powerhouse and resulted in a population used to engaging in civil society discourse and participating in protests. Tens of thousands have taken part in the ''Umbrella Movement,'' and the Tiananmen Square Massacre's 25th anniversary demonstration drew 200,000. Many of the pro-democracy movement's strongest voices are its youngest.

A third sign from events in Hong Kong is just how pivotal a moment this is. Will Hong Kong's leaders address the current impasse

in Hong Kong and will it retain its current unique place as a financial center or, as my colleague here says, just become another Chinese city wracked with corruption and censorship.

More importantly, I would like to call attention to what events in Hong Kong signal for human rights more generally in China. Well, they signal continued repression in mainland China. If the CCP won't tolerate previously agreed-upon universal suffrage in Hong Kong, a region protected by the international covenant on civil and political rights, they surely will not undertake any meaningful democratic reforms on the mainland, and they are signaling to their population that there will be consequences for any similar protests in China.

Escalating anxiety within the CCP, increased anti-foreign rhetoric and more stringent censorship on the mainland are emerging. Uniting citizens behind a common foreign enemy is a popular CCP smokescreen. Even as the United States and China are agreeing to reduce greenhouse gas emissions and cut tariffs, Chinese leaders are calling on other nations to challenge U.S. hegemony on the Internet, targeting U.S. companies for investigation, and praising anti-American writers.

The CCP's anxiety isn't unfounded. The people of China hunger for democracy. That hunger still exists despite all the odds. Despite the CCP's strict control of media and the Internet and despite the fact that supporting or sharing information about protests has resulted in dozens of arrests on the mainland, there is an appetite for narratives to challenge one-party rule.

Well, I imagine what you want to hear most from me is what steps the United States and the international community should take to support democracy and human rights in Hong Kong and China. First, the international community should publicly support the people of Hong Kong. A newly published report by Freedom House called ''Supporting Democracy Abroad'' found that in U.S. foreign policy toward China, ''Immediate economic and strategic interests almost always override support for democracy and human rights.'' That needs to change.

Second, multilateral efforts are important. They should include a UN resolution urging Hong Kong authorities to fully implement the ICCPR, a visit to Hong Kong by the UN Special Rapporteur on the Rights to Freedom of Peaceful Assembly and of Association, resolutions by democratic nations like our own in support of Hong Kong citizens determining their own future, and efforts to identify points of economic leverage that would pressure Chinese authorities to respect Hong Kong's special status. I would be happy to talk about it a bit more.

Congress can play a powerful role. I commend you for both S. 2922 and H.R. 5696, for taking steps such as renewing Section 301 of the U.S.–Hong Kong Policy Act to reinstate regular reports to Congress on the development of democratic institutions in Hong Kong, maintaining vigorous Radio Free Asia and Voice of America broadcasting in Cantonese, and tying any U.S. differential treatment of Hong Kong relative to China to Hong Kong's autonomy.

When I was a House leadership staffer—as I close here—during the 1997 handover, one might well have asked, ''Will Hong Kong infect that the rest of China with its freedoms or will China infect

Hong Kong with its lack of them?'' We have a crucial moment here to see the likely future of freedom in Hong Kong and in China as a whole. The Chinese people are watching and it is no time for self-respecting democratic nations to be coy and muted.

Thank you very much.

Chairman BROWN. Thank you, Ambassador.

Dr. Bush, welcome.

RICHARD C. BUSH III, PH.D., SENIOR FELLOW; DIRECTOR, CENTER FOR EAST ASIA POLICY STUDIES; CHEN–FU AND CECILIA YEN KOO CHAIR IN TAIWAN STUDIES, THE BROOKINGS INSTITUTION

Mr. BUSH. Thank you very much. Chairman Brown, Chairman Smith, thank you for giving me the privilege to testify today. Thank you for your leadership on this issue.

I have four general themes. Theme number one, Hong Kong is important to the United States and to U.S.-China relations primarily because it is a test of the proposition that ethnic Chinese people are perfectly capable of democratic citizenship. I do believe they are and I believe that democratic success in Hong Kong strengthens the hand of political reformers in China over the long term.

A democratic system in Hong Kong should be first, representative in that candidates for major elections offer voters a choice among major points of view. Second, accountable in that citizens, through elections, may confer legitimacy on leaders who do well and fire those who do not. And third, effective: the majority of Hong Kong people no doubt want a democratic system for its own stake, but they also expect that it would address the problems in their everyday lives.

There are other American interests at play in Hong Kong. There are 1,200 American companies and about 60,000 American expatriates there. Many U.S. residents of Hong Kong origin live in the United States and make significant contributions to our society. Still it is Hong Kong's political future that is most important to U.S. interests.

Theme number two, the U.S.-Hong Kong Policy Act remains a sound foundation for American policy. Its prescriptions remain valid and its emphasis on preserving Hong Kong's autonomy in areas critical to U.S. interests is more important today than it was in 1992.

Regarding the bill you've introduced, Mr. Chairmen, I support the resumption of the State Department reports on Hong Kong. Actually, it would be a good and timely signal for the administration to resume the reports without waiting for legislation. But periodic congressional hearings on Hong Kong are also needed.

I am agnostic on your proposal to require the President to certify that Hong Kong is sufficiently autonomous before any new laws, agreements, and arrangements are applied to it. That requirement is certainly implicit in the original law. Even with certification, substantive consultations between the two branches on this matter would be useful.

Theme number three, what has happened in Hong Kong in the last three months was not foreordained. There was a compromise available earlier this year on how to elect Hong Kong's Chief Executive, one that would likely have assured a competitive election.

The decision of the PRC's National People's Congress Standing Committee on August 31 ignored relevant and moderate Hong Kong proposals along these lines. Many in Hong Kong, therefore, concluded that the nominating committee would be a new way for Beijing to deny them a competitive election, so they have used the only tool available, public protests.

The protest movement was assuredly about ensuring generally competitive elections and representative government, but it was also fueled by widespread public dissatisfaction over inequality of income, wealth, job opportunities, and access to affordable housing.

Fourth, the protest movement has not been perfect in the way it has carried out its campaign. It lacked unity and an exit strategy, but it appears that at least some of the leaders now understand the need to stand down, along the lines that Governor Patten was suggesting.

Fifth, even within the parameters laid down by Beijing, it may be possible to engineer a nominating process that has a competitive character and senior Hong Kong officials have hinted as much.

Theme number four: the U.S. Government, I think, has pursued a skillful threading of the policy needle and it should continue to do so. The Administration has been measured, clear, balanced, and pointed in its rhetorical statements on the current situation. I would refer you, in particular, to the White House statement of September 29, which clearly signaled American support for a genuinely democratic solution.

Concerning a Chinese charge that the U.S. Government is the ''Black Hand'' behind the current protest movement, nothing could be further from the truth. I am pleased that President Obama authoritatively made clear to President Xi Jinping last week that the Hong Kong protest movement was totally homegrown. Taking Chinese paranoia into account should not be a reason not to act.

Finally, our diplomats in Hong Kong are skilled professionals who understand both the promise and problems of the current situation. They understand what all of us should appreciate and that is the need to hear a range of Hong Kong views and a range does exist. There are sensible people in both the establishment and the democratic camp, people who understand the need to address all of Hong Kong's governance problems through a political system that is representative, accountable, and effective and we should take our cues from such people.

Thank you very much.

Chairman BROWN. Thank you very much, Dr. Bush.

Congressman Smith will begin the questions.

Representative SMITH. Thank you very much, Chairman, for that courtesy extended.

Let me thank all three of you for your extraordinary testimonies and for years of service providing insight and counsel and commentary that is incisive and actionable. I do want to note before I go to a couple of questions that Dr. Yang Jianli is here who has testified previously in front of some of my committees in the past

and Harry Wu as well, two unbelievably brave and brilliant men who have paid with their lives, with their freedom in terms of time in incarceration in the laogai.

Dr. Yang from 2000 to 2007, a signer of Charter '08 and Harry Wu, two decades. I have read Harry's writings. I have been to his Laogai Museum which chronicles the abuses of Beijing against the dissidents and religious believers and of course, democracy activists. Having them present today is a reminder of what many in Hong Kong may face.

I remember having—and I won't mention his name, because it might put a further a target on his back—but in the 1990s having dinner with a leader in Hong Kong who said he expected some day to be in prison. This was after the agreement with the UK, of course, and Beijing and he expected to be in prison.

I think, as you said Ambassador Lagon, that we are at a pivotal moment and we should not be coy and muted. I thought that was a very fine way of putting it. Business as usual does not cut it. I remember after Tiananmen Square when President Clinton made a very strong statement and actually issued an Executive Order saying that most-favored-nation [MFN] status—which the Chinese Government relied on—was a goner unless there was significant progress in human rights.

I gave press conferences backing President Clinton, was behind him 100 percent only to learn that it was a false statement being made by the President and even halfway through the review period, made a trip to Beijing—this would've been about 1992—met with members of the Chamber of Commerce who kept saying we want MFN regardless of what the human rights situation was. Of course on May 26, 1994, the President ripped up his own Executive Order and that was the end of the linkage of human rights and a trading relationship with the People's Republic of China.

Let's not make that mistake again with Hong Kong. The good people of Hong Kong understand freedom, as do the people of the mainland, of course. They have lived it. The Basic Law protects them and I hope that we are not coy and muted, Mr. Ambassador, as you pointed out and do let Beijing know that we mean business this time.

Maybe the three of you might comment on whether or not we have shown the seriousness, the sense that we mean what we say, and we are behind the "Umbrella Movement." I'm glad you pointed out a moment ago, Mr. Bush, that none of this came from the United States or the international community and as Lord Patten said, it is a slur to suggest that the people of Hong Kong are not doing this because they believe in democracy and human rights and want their Basic Law enshrined in perpetuity in that country.

In your opening comments, Ambassador Lagon, you talked about how Hong Kong is a party to the ICCPR, the International Covenant for Civil and Political Rights, and that China is only a signatory. Part of the subterfuge coming out of Beijing for years was that every time somebody was making their way, some high leader from China, President, Premier, we always hear about they are just ready to sign the international covenant and then they signed it but never ratified it. So there was always that sense of, oh, there is some kind of transition occurring. Of course, it was always a

false promise because they certainly have not lived up to any of it—that goes for the Torture Convention or anything else.

Touch on that, if you will, if we have been shown—I asked Lord Patten about Hu Jintao and Xi Jinping, whether or not there has been a change. We know that Xi Jinping has some kind of strange fascination, if not respect, for the egregious abuses of Mao Zedong.

Have we seen a further embark on repressiveness on the part of Beijing and I have other questions, but I think in the time, that will do.

Ambassador LAGON. I thank you very much for your questions and the premises behind it. I would say, generally speaking, that the United States will be blamed by Chinese authorities for being behind those who are calling for freedom. If that is the case, particularly in recent weeks in Hong Kong, then the United States should be plain. If it is going to be accused of being behind a totally indigenous civil society movement that is largely peaceful in its activity, the United States should not only make firm, quiet statements behind the scenes, but publicly stand with those who would like to see the promises made in the past about a move toward more direct democratic elections come about.

I would emphasize asking "who is destabilizing here?" It is destabilizing if the United States is quiet and doesn't stand up for the principles that it believes in and, indeed, stand up for those things that the Chinese have promised.

You asked about the ICCPR, and I think it reveals an important distinction between Hong Kong and China; we should be careful not to see a hard crackdown on corruption as something that is grounded in due process and rule of law. Some admire efforts to fight corruption, but it really is targeted against particularly unfavored political figures in China.

It doesn't represent the broader rule of law that the ICCPR would envision. We should watch Hong Kong to see whether the grounding it has had living up to the basic liberties of the ICCPR is actually seeping away.

Mr. BUSH. Thank you for the question. I think that we should continue to express public views about the situation in Hong Kong and where it is going. President Obama essentially promised Xi Jinping that we would be doing that in spite of Xi's preference that we not.

I know Congressman Smith, Senator Brown, that you understand the People's Republic of China very well and that if the leadership has decided that it is not going to grant genuine democracy, it will not do it. The history of the negotiations with Britain, I think, revealed a very rigid approach by China to keeping things the way they wanted.

I think one of the reasons they are taking a rigid approach now is that they fear the message in China of another democratic Chinese system on its periphery. Having one in Taiwan is bad enough, having another in Hong Kong just leads to people inside China asking the question why not us too. That is incendiary.

I think one of the things that we should be doing going forward is to be alert to essentially covert Chinese efforts to restrict what freedoms remain: Freedom of the press, the rule of law, the activi-

ties of civil society, and so on. There are ways that restrictions could be imposed and unless we are alert, we will not see them.

I would conclude by saying that if China wants to preserve the current power structure and system in Hong Kong, it is going to continue to have trouble. The commitment to democracy, the sense of political alienation from the status quo is extremely strong. Even if this protest movement packs up and goes home, is only temporary.

Thank you.

Ms. HUI. I want to make sure that I do not really comment on U.S. foreign policy, but I do want to say one thing: international attention to Hong Kong is very important.

People were really shocked that the police would fire tear gas and 87 rounds. But people were equally shocked that the police suddenly stopped after firing 87 rounds.

Why? Because, probably, some people realized that the whole world was watching. There were all of these international reporters, actually, covering the event live. So I think it is very important that the world continues to pay attention to what is going on in Hong Kong.

With regard to the question about Xi Jinping's position on Hong Kong, I want to just relay what actually Albert Chen said. Albert Chen was, actually, on the Basic Law drafting committee and he is also considered as one of those who really has a close ear to Beijing.

He said in a program—letter to Hong Kong—that the problem for Hong Kong is that in the 1980s the expectation was that there should be convergence between the mainland system and the Hong Kong system over time. This is why there were all these promises. Then why 50 years having no changes?

But over time, and especially under Xi Jinping, the Chinese system, the mainland system has become increasingly authoritarian. Therefore, Beijing cannot tolerate for Hong Kong to become more democratic. I think this is actually a very good insight coming from someone who knows what Beijing thinks.

Senator BROWN. Thank you, Chairman Smith.

Dr. Hui, let me start with you. You informed us that you were in Hong Kong observing the protests. Understanding the news reports, understanding always mixed reaction in any country in the world when there are protests, mixed reaction within the country— could you give us your observations and description of how you believe the rest of Hong Kong society responded to the protests, those people who weren't on the streets, those people who weren't family members—however you want to segment your response in terms of what kind of people had what kind of responses and reactions to the protests?

Ms. HUI. As I said earlier, I think really the dividing line is whether people believe that we can continue to preserve freedom without democracy. I think this really divides people.

And even for myself, for someone in my generation—the problem is that people like me, we grew up in a Hong Kong that really enjoyed freedom without democracy. So a lot of these people wonder what is the fuss, what are these students doing?

It is also interesting to see this major generation gap. So young people are overwhelmingly supportive of the Occupy movement. They really want to have a say in shaping their own future. Whereas the older people, and often even their own parents, are really anti-occupy. And a lot of——

Chairman BROWN. Break that down. I understand young people are more likely—that's probably fairly typical of protests, always knowing that. Was it broken down, in part, by class, those who are the most successful people materially in Hong Kong, are they most likely to oppose them? Is it broken down at all by education or broken at all by race? What are your thoughts?

Ms. HUI. It is partially broken down by class because the richest and most famous of Hong Kong people, they are almost always pro-regime. I think that is true. But at the same time, I really think that this is an across-class movement. It is a cross-class movement because it actually has been going on for 30 years. So you have all of these professionals, you have actually upper-middle-class people who all want democracy.

Now some of these people, even when they really want democracy, they still disagree with the Occupy movement because this is a disruptive action. It is unprecedented in Hong Kong's history. So for a lot of these people, while yes, we like democracy but we really don't want to cause disruption to Hong Kong's businesses. That is one thing.

But otherwise, it really comes down to the generation gap. People who are young, who have a good education are overwhelmingly supportive of the movement, however, and in whatever forms of resistance people take. Whereas, older people can be a bit divided.

Some of them can really be, "Okay, so what that we don't have democracy or we like democracy, but we should fight for it through other means."

Chairman BROWN. How do you define young, under 35, under 30?

Ms. HUI. Probably under 25, yes.

Chairman BROWN. Under 25.

Ms. HUI. Because even the latest polls show that when there are more and more people who don't really want the students to stay on the streets, we still see that people under age 25, they are still overwhelmingly supportive of the Occupy movement.

Chairman BROWN. Is there resentment of older, not necessarily wealthy Hong Kong people, but older—well specifically this, is there resentment from older, sort of, working-class Hong Kong people that these are privileged students that ought to get a job and go out and contribute to society rather than protesting? Do you see that kind of class division?

Ms. HUI. I don't see that. I actually see the workers really behind the movement. Again it is important to see that the "Umbrella Movement" didn't just start two months ago. This is just one episode in a 30-year-long democracy movement.

So one day when the police tried to take away all of the obstacles, the roadblocks, then there were these construction workers that showed up with all of this bamboo—in Hong Kong when you have construction sites, you have these bamboos. Actually, you use

bamboo in order to fix all of the buildings outside. And they set up new barricades with these bamboo sticks.

So this is really a cross-class movement. And also workers, especially for example, a little while ago workers were also protesting against unfair treatment and that was actually the first time that a movement against Li Ka-shing, the richest person in Hong Kong, had really broad support.

So I would really say that this is a cross-class movement. Students are at the forefront, but they are supported by the traditional pan-democrats, they are supported by workers, they are supported by professionals. Among these people who support democracy, there may be some division over tactics, strategies, but I think there is broad support for democracy in Hong Kong.

Chairman BROWN. So the bamboo scaffolding was used as barriers.

Ms. HUI. Yes, for a day.

Chairman BROWN. Thank you.

Ambassador Lagon, you spoke of points of economic leverage to pressure China on Hong Kong. Could you be specific, what points of economic pressure, how you would use them, how we should exercise them, and who should exercise them?

Ambassador LAGON. Well, I thank you for that question and I think it relates both to our relationship with China—economically, broadly—and with Hong Kong. I think it is an excellent provision in your legislation that you have recently introduced to have a Presidential certification so that for any preferential treatment, which often has commercial, trade, or technology transfer, elements, there is a certification about whether autonomy is actually veritably in place. That is a form of leverage.

Let me just speak more broadly about leverage with China. The common statement is that China is the United States' banker and that there is a substantial trade deficit that the United States has with China. I am puzzled by the degree to which people think that means China has all of the leverage. We should have China's attention.

We should engage them and I know that businesses today do not say what they said when I was a House staffer in 1997, that somehow bathing China in commercial relations is going to wash away the dictatorship like a universal solvent. We should try and use that leverage.

Chairman BROWN. That is so interesting because I was in the House with Congressman Smith then and I remember the arguments from America's largest corporations that we would turn China into a democracy by shutting production down in Steubenville and Dayton, Ohio, and moving it to Wuhan and Xi'an and then selling products back into the United States, a business plan followed by so many American businesses large enough to do them.

I also remember and I think Dr. Bush remembers this, that a friend of mine said that there were more corporate jets at National Airport during the lead up to PNTR [permanent normal trade relations] and CEOs that normally would not deal individually with House Members were even going to the fifth floor of Cannon in those days to talk to House Members and lobby on something where they consistently told us they wanted access to a million

Chinese consumers when they really wanted access to hundreds of millions of Chinese workers.

So we have our leverage points if we care to use them, understanding American business interests in China don't necessarily want to use them. Comments on that?

Ambassador LAGON. If I can make an added point, I was on the floor of the Senate when the vote happened on PNTR, when precious few Senators voted against, but not only has political reform not taken place in mainland China, but let's look at slippage and Hong Kong, the subject of your hearing today.

The benchmarks of the Freedom House ''Freedom of the Press'' report are very disturbing. There is slippage in press freedom—what one most closely associates with civil liberties—in Hong Kong because of pressures from Beijing directly or from media owners, of self-censorship, and of an increase in physical attacks, quite brutal, against journalists there.

But the biggest benchmark is a human one. The first Chief Civil Servant under Chinese sovereignty in Hong Kong, Anson Chang, has become a very prominent critic of the way things have slid in Hong Kong and is very concerned about where things have unfolded on the question of elections.

Chairman BROWN. Thank you.

Dr. Bush, you mentioned fears among the highest echelons of the Chinese Government that Hong Kong would look a little bit too much like Taiwan in terms of democracy. I remember I met with—maybe 10 years ago—a number of the top Chinese leaders. There was a congressional delegation of a half-dozen of us.

The thing that exercised their top leadership the most and impassioned them the most was not labor protests and there were dozens of those a week throughout a country of, at that point, 1.1, 1.2 billion. What bothered them the most was the mention of Taiwan. So your experience, obviously, rings true to that.

Tell me how these protests in Hong Kong—what effect they've had: one, in Taiwan; and second, what effect they've had with cross-strait relations?

Mr. BUSH. Thanks for the question. With respect to the impact on Taiwan, it is my impression, having been in Taiwan right after I was in Hong Kong, was that after the initial media coverage of the Hong Kong situation, public attention in Taiwan was diverted to other issues and there were serious issues. I would say that for Taiwan people what has happened in Hong Kong and what is likely to happen in Hong Kong only confirm the long-held belief that the two entities should not be treated under the same framework as China is trying to do, that China's application of ''one country, two systems'' in Hong Kong just proves why it is inappropriate for Taiwan. This is a major obstacle to the PRC achieving its political objectives with respect to Taiwan.

I'm not sure there has been a huge impact——

Chairman BROWN. Let me explore that for a second. Sorry to interrupt. So if news reports which suggest that President Ma is certainly, in contrast to Chen Shui-bian, friendlier to China and wanting to establish more cross-border relationships and if the next step of that is that Taiwan is moving more toward—without overstating

this—some kind of Chinese model, does this play up on that? Do the issues of democracy in Hong Kong push back on that?

Mr. BUSH. Well I think it contributes to a trend that is already in play and that is that the Ma administration and China have grabbed all of the low-hanging fruit in terms of the sorts of cooperation that they can get and Taiwan politics was immobilized earlier this year, as you recall, by a similar protest movement that took over the legislature because of public unhappiness about a trade and services agreement that the Ma administration had negotiated.

Moreover, where China would really like to go on cross-strait relations is political talks. President Ma has correctly been very wary of going down that road because he is very committed to the idea of the Republic of China. And that is something that Beijing really doesn't want to talk about.

I would also note that President Ma, who was actually born in Hong Kong, came out a few weeks ago with a very strong statement in favor of democracy in Hong Kong and the peaceful protests that were going on. Beijing was profoundly unhappy with his statement and felt that he was sticking his nose where it didn't belong, but he, I think, was very pleased that he did that.

Chairman BROWN. Was that a surprise to KMT [Kuomintang] members that President Ma would do that?

Mr. BUSH. I frankly don't know. President Ma has been always very forthright about the need for democracy in China and also in Hong Kong. So perhaps they weren't surprised.

Chairman BROWN. One last question about that, did the protest in Taiwan, at least in part, serve as a template for what happened in Hong Kong?

Mr. BUSH. I know there was a lot of interaction between activists in Taiwan and activists in Hong Kong, exchanging experiences and techniques and so on. I went to one of the protest areas in Hong Kong one evening that I was there and there was a gentleman talking to a small crowd and he was clearly not a Hong Kong person.

He was from Taiwan. He was speaking very good Mandarin which is the language of instruction there, talking about the situation in Taiwan. So there is some interaction. This, of course, could play into the PRC narrative that there are a bunch of Black Hands, the United States, Taiwan, and so on. But the Hong Kong protests are definitely homegrown.

Chairman BROWN. Thank you. Professor Hui, thank you. Ambassador Lagon, thank you. Dr. Bush, thank you.

If you have further comments, please send them to the Commission by Monday, if you could. There is some chance that some members of the Commission that either couldn't be here or Congressman Pittenger or Senator Cardin or Congressman Smith will have written questions for you. If you would get those answers back to the Commission as quickly as possible. So thank you all for your willingness to speak out.

Mr. BUSH. Thank you for the opportunity.

[Whereupon, at 4:39 p.m., the hearing was concluded.]

APPENDIX

PREPARED STATEMENT OF VICTORIA TIN-BOR HUI

NOVEMBER 20, 2014

Testimony by Victoria Tin-bor Hui

Victoria Tin-bor Hui, Ph.D.: Associate Professor, Department of Political Science; Faculty Fellow, Liu Institute for Asia and Asian Studies, University of Notre Dame.

Though I am originally from Hong Kong, I am speaking today as an academic expert. I do not claim to speak for protestors who have faced down police force and thug violence—they have been speaking for themselves in numerous channels. I only wish to highlight the significance of what they have been doing.

The protestors' demand is easily summarized by a yellow banner that can be seen everywhere in Hong Kong: "We want genuine universal suffrage (我要真普選)." This refers to the right to nominate candidates as well as the right to vote for the next Chief Executive in 2017.

The Umbrella Movement has seen hundreds of thousands of protestors occupying busy streets. At the same time, the local and international media have shown images of counter-protestors roughing up non-violent protesters.

The division among Hong Kong people hinges on one question: Is it possible to preserve freedom without democracy? Hong Kong people, whether they are pro-occupy or anti-occupy, cherish freedom. They want a neutral civil service, an impartial police, an independent judiciary, and a free press. These core values have been eroded in the absence of democracy. Freedom is fast disappearing without democracy.

Hong Kong has seen three Chief Executives since 1997. They were chosen by a narrowly-based Election Committee beholden to Beijing and have successively undercut Hong Kong's core values.[1]

The first Chief Executive, C. H. Tung, under Beijing prodding, introduced a draconian national security bill in 2003. He was forced to shelve the bill and then resign after half a million protesters took to the streets. With the Umbrella Movement, pro-establishment politicians are talking about re-introducing the national security bill.

The second Chief Executive, Donald Tsang, introduced political appointments. Without electoral accountability, this practice created cronyism and eroded the meritocratic and impersonal civil service.

The third and current Chief Executive, CY Leung, has stepped up the appointments of his loyal supporters to key government positions and advisory committees. His extensive appointments of business and political friends have further undermined public accountability and corrupted the government. Under his watch, even the Independent Commission Against Corruption has become the target of a corruption investigation, as testified by the investigation of the former Commissioner Timothy Tong. To make matters worse, CY Leung has been accused of receiving payouts of HK$50 million and then $37 million from the Australian firm UGL without publicly reporting them. In addition, the police have come under attack for arbitrary arrests of protestors

and selective enforcement of the law. Media critics of the government have been demoted or fired, with some journalists subjected to physical attacks by thugs.

The rapid erosion of freedom in the past two years has seriously undercut Hong Kong's promised autonomy. Protestors want genuine universal suffrage because the previous system of "freedom without democracy" is broken.

Some HK people, many in my generation and older, long believed that Hong Kong could keep its freedom without democracy. But this view goes against world experience.[2] It is not coincidental that Hong Kong has been the only case of "freedom without democracy" in the world -- and this unique case is fast disappearing. All around the world, freedom and democracy are either present together or absent together, strong together or weak together. It is simply impossible to preserve a meritocratic civil service, an impartial police, an independent judiciary, and a free press in an undemocratic setting.

Protestors are loud and clear about their goal of the promised genuine universal suffrage. But it is not easy to get there.

The Umbrella Movement is nearing the end of the second month. As the government has refused to have a meaningful dialogue with protestors, supporters are looking for alternative ways to sustain the movement beyond occupying busy streets. It may be less daunting, though by no means easy, to put pressure on business elites who are in the position to influence Beijing's decision. All over the world, business elites are naturally pro-regime. But they may have second thoughts if protestors can impose costs on their continued collusion with the government.

Toward that end, protestors are circulating a growing list of businesses for a targeted boycott.[3] The government plans to turn the 1200-member Election Committee into a nominating committee for the Chief Executive in 2017. Leading members of this committee are Hong Kong's richest tycoons who dominate most businesses that affect everyone's daily life. Hong Kong's rich and famous may be convinced that keeping the economy open to the world depends on guarding Hong Kong's freedom with democracy. An open and vibrant Hong Kong will surely serve their long-term interests better than securing short-term deals and contracts in Beijing.

Ultimately, it is incumbent on the Hong Kong government to address protestors' demand. As bailiffs are clearing occupy sites this week, the government may be tempted to think that the problem will simply go away. But the source of the problem is not the occupy movement; it is the government's erosion of freedom.[4] Protestors will continue the struggle for genuine universal suffrage with other forms of civil disobedience. Now that the government has also trained an Umbrella generation to be fearless in the face of criminal arrests, police force and thug violence, any repressive measures will only drive hundreds of thousands back to the street. The government has no alternative but to reopen the consultation process on electoral arrangements.

HK's student leaders say that history has chosen them—students have admirably shouldered this burden of history. History has also chosen HK's powerful adults to make right choices.

●　————————————

[1] Hong Kong is not unlike other world cases in which political incumbents are responsible for the erosion of

●————————————————————————————

freedom and democracy. See Juan Linz and Alfred Stepan, eds., *Breakdown of Democratic Regimes*, Baltimore: Johns Hopkins University Press, 1978.

[2] See Douglass C. North, John Joseph Wallis, Barry R Weingast, *Violence and Social Orders: A Conceptual Framework for Interpreting Recorded Human History*, Cambridge University Press, 2009; Edward D. Mansfield, Jack L. Snyder, "Democratic Transitions, Institutional Strength, and War," *International Organization*, Volume 56, Number 2, Spring 2002, pp. 297-337; Brian D. Taylor, *State Building in Putin's Russia: Policing and Coercion after Communism*, Cambridge University Press, 2011.

[3] The boycott list (《全港不合作運動 - 抵制建制派商戶大行動》抵制商戶名單) is available at https://docs.google.com/spreadsheets/d/1NRermxQ6CzkBbAr9v8taH9F0-8R6P-vmsE2qCZhkXGU/htmlview?sle=true.

[4] In academic language, the Hong Kong government is responsible for "constructing" the Umbrella Movement. See Jeff Goodwin, *No Other Way Out*, Cambridge University Press, 2001; Charles Tilly and Sidney Tarrow, *Contentious Politics*, Oxford University Press, 2006.

————————

PREPARED STATEMENT OF MARK P. LAGON

NOVEMBER 20, 2014

THE UMBRELLA MOVEMENT: A PIVOTAL MOMENT FOR DEMOCRACY IN HONG KONG

INTRODUCTION

Chairman Brown, Co-chairman Smith, and distinguished members of the Commission, it is an honor to appear before you today.

We have reached a pivotal moment for the future of democracy in Hong Kong. As you know, Hong Kong and China are very different.

Hong Kong is a party to the International Covenant on Civil and Political Rights (ICCPR); China is only a signatory. Hong Kong is ranked Partly Free in Freedom House's *Freedom in the World* report for 2014; China is ranked Not Free. Hong Kong is ranked Partly Free in Freedom House's *Freedom of the Press* report for 2014; China is ranked Not Free.

These differences provide important context for my remarks today, which focus on the significance of the protests in Hong Kong for human rights in Hong Kong and in China.

Despite the fact that Hong Kong's Basic Law guarantees one country with two systems until 2047, Chinese officials continue to redefine and reinterpret the law. Article 45 of the Basic Law states that, "the ultimate aim is the selection of the Chief Executive by universal suffrage upon nomination by a broadly representative nominating committee in accordance with democratic procedures." [1] In 2007, the National People's Congress Standing Committee (NPCSC) ruled that the first universal suffrage election for Chief Executive could take place in 2017. Yet, in August 2014, the NPCSC reversed course, instead deciding that the next Chief Executive must be elected from a pre-selected pool of candidates.

Article 27 of the Basic Law guarantees the freedoms of speech, press, and publication. Yet, when Hong Kongers took to the streets to protest the August NPCSC ruling, police did nothing to protect them from thuggish attacks by CCP supporters, instead responding aggressively and tear-gassing the crowd. Images of peaceful protesters fending off tear gas with only umbrellas to protect themselves generated the movement's iconic name: the Umbrella Revolution. The aggressive police response was especially troubling, because the demonstrators had taken no violent action and because the aggression was a clear violation of the right to peaceably assemble— a right long protected in Hong Kong. Many were arrested, including a key student leader of the movement, Joshua Wong. Wong was detained for more than forty hours and was released after his lawyers filed a habeas corpus petition—a petition option that does not exist in China.

Optimists have long hoped that because of Hong Kong's economic strength and regional importance, China would follow through with its commitment to the "one country, two systems" arrangement to which it committed until 2047. Many have even hoped that the Xi presidency would usher in an era of meaningful democratic

————————

[1] *The Basic Law*, http://www.basiclaw.gov.hk/en/basiclawtext/chapter—4.html#section—1

reform in China. Unfortunately, the events in Hong Kong have provided a clear answer to the contrary in both cases.

WHAT DO THE EVENTS IN HONG KONG SIGNAL FOR HUMAN RIGHTS IN HONG KONG SPECIFICALLY?

1. A continued push by China to assume ultimate control of Hong Kong. I believe we will see China continue to reinterpret and redefine existing law to exert ever-increasing control and influence over Hong Kong, which could negatively impact human rights. We have already seen freedoms in Hong Kong slowly declining since the handover in 1997. Press freedom is at its lowest point in a decade; Beijing has attempted to introduce a propagandistic "national education" curriculum in Hong Kong schools; and the white paper released by Beijing in June 2014 affirming the CCP's "comprehensive jurisdiction" over the region stated that all city administrators—including judges—must "love China."[2] Many believe circumstances will only get worse as 2047 approaches. The 1200 member nominating committee assigned with vetting candidates for the next chief executive election will be based on the current election committee, which is comprised of a variety of special interests and is disproportionately weighted with pro-CCP members. Because they perceive that it is within their interests to do so, the majority of Hong Kong's political and economic elite side with the CCP on most matters, and would likely be willing to cede additional controls to Beijing so long as it does not interfere with their status.

2. Strong popular support for democracy and universal human rights that is not likely to disappear. Hong Kongers have experienced a starkly different history from their mainland neighbors over the last hundred years, a history of rule of law rooted in a respect for universal rights. It is precisely this tradition of rights-based law that has enabled Hong Kong to become an economic powerhouse and resulted in a population used to actively engaging in civil society discourse. There are civil society organizations addressing a wide range of issues, including political rights, health care, the environment, women's political participation, LGBTI rights, religion, and even arts and culture and sports. Hong Kongers are also experienced with protests. Tens of thousands have participated in Umbrella Movement protests. Tens of thousands also turn out for the Tiananmen Square Massacre protest vigil, which has been held in Hong Kong each year since 1989. The 2014 event commemorating the massacre's 25th anniversary drew a crowd of nearly two hundred thousand. Hong Kongers have also marched to commemorate the anniversary of the handover, to support democracy, and to oppose pro-CCP school curriculum changes and national security laws. Many of the pro-democracy movement's strongest voices are also its youngest voices. They are highly digitally literate, and since Hong Kong has the world's third-fastest Internet speeds, they are able to communicate instantaneously worldwide. Given these factors, support for democracy and human rights in Hong Kong is not likely to be silenced any time soon.

3. A pivotal moment for Hong Kong. As both sides dig in their heels and we hear reported plans by the Hong Kong government to remove the remaining protesters, democracy in Hong Kong is reaching a pivotal moment. It will be very difficult to maintain the "one country, two systems" arrangement and sustain Hong Kong's economic prosperity without addressing the public's demands for democracy. If Hong Kong's leaders—influenced by Beijing—ultimately reject democratic demands and move toward more mainland-style policies, Hong Kong's special status will be put at risk. The way they choose to address the current impasse will factor heavily into whether the "one country, two systems" set-up can work and whether Hong Kong will retain its unique place as a financial center in Asia, or whether over time its prosperity will decline as it becomes just another Chinese city, racked with corruption, censorship, and pollution.

WHAT DO THE EVENTS IN HONG KONG SIGNAL FOR HUMAN RIGHTS IN CHINA?

1. Continued repression in mainland China. Following the handover in 1997, optimists had hoped that Hong Kong's freedom and prosperity would trickle into China. The ongoing events in Hong Kong signal that, unfortunately, the opposite is true. China's authoritarianism is trickling into Hong Kong. Much of what the CCP does is with an eye to its domestic audience. If the current CCP leadership will not tolerate previously agreed upon universal suffrage in Hong Kong—a region protected by the International Covenant on Civil and Political Rights—they certainly will not undertake any meaningful democratic reforms on the mainland. They

---

[2] "Full text: Chinese State Council white paper on 'One Country, Two Systems' policy in Hong Kong," *South China Morning Post,* 10 June 2014, http://www.scmp.com/news/hong-kong/article/1529167/full-text-practice-one-country-two-systems-policy-hong-kong-special.

are also signaling that mainland Chinese should not expect democratic participation either. And, by having state media condemn and discredit protesters in Hong Kong, CCP leaders are also signaling to mainlanders that there will be consequences for any similar protests in China. The CCP has no plans to allow space for civil society, respect for universal human rights, or any weakening of their control over the Chinese people's voice, and the events in Hong Kong will only strengthen their resolve to strictly maintain that control.

2. Escalating anxiety within the CCP, which has resulted in increased antiforeign rhetoric and more stringent censorship on the mainland. As recently noted in *The New York Times,* "the vilification of foreigners as enemies of China has been a staple of propaganda by the Communist Party since before its rise to power, [but] analysts say the leadership tends to ramp up such rhetoric when it feels under pressure at home." Uniting citizens behind a common foreign enemy has been a popular CCP smokescreen for decades, distracting citizens from the corruption, pollution, and lack of free expression that plague the mainland. The latest round of anti-American rhetoric has been marked. Even as the United States and China are agreeing to reduce greenhouse gas emissions and cut tariffs for technology products, Chinese leaders are calling on other nations to "challenge U.S. hegemony on the Internet," targeting U.S. companies for investigation, and praising anti-American Chinese writers. This type of rhetoric can have broad implications for future relations, disrupting cooperation, information sharing, and even trade relations. The CCP is also working hard to block and control traditional and social media coverage of Hong Kong. According to Freedom House's forthcoming *Freedom on the Net* report, which will be released on December 4, CCP censorship efforts in China during October 2014 were even more intense than in June 2014, which was the 25th anniversary of the Tiananmen Square Massacre.

3. The CCP's anxiety is not unfounded, because hunger for democracy still exists within China, despite the odds. Hong Kong's protests have been successful because of their scale and the international attention they have garnered, generating significant interest in China. Despite the CCP's strict control of traditional media and sophisticated Internet censorship, mainland Chinese have still been able to unearth coverage of the Umbrella Movement. And, despite the fact that sharing information about the protests or expressing support for them is forbidden and has resulted in dozens of arrests and detentions, mainland Chinese are still sharing information and still expressing support. Activists in China have used digital technology to evade censorship and risked their personal security to discuss the protests. Though many in China who speak publicly about the protests have expressed strong opposition, there is a curiosity about and appetite for narratives that challenge one party rule. Some mainland Chinese tourists in Hong Kong at the time of the protests went to watch the demonstrations, though China has since suspended approval of tours to Hong Kong. The Umbrella Movement had provided mainland prodemocracy advocates an opportunity to witness widespread international support for democracy efforts in the People's Republic of China.

WHAT STEPS CAN THE UNITED STATES AND THE INTERNATIONAL COMMUNITY TAKE TO SUPPORT DEMOCRACY AND HUMAN RIGHTS IN HONG KONG AND CHINA?

1. The international community—including the United States—should publicly support the aspirations of the people of Hong Kong. It is the right thing to do both morally and pragmatically. There is always great debate about whether foreign expressions of support for democracy movements will endanger the movement and its participants—a so-called "kiss of death"—and the Hong Kong case is no different. The CCP has a long history of blaming "foreign hostile forces" for any popular movement it does not like, and CCP leaders have taken every opportunity to do so during the Hong Kong protests. These bully tactics should not prevent the international community from speaking out to support the right of all Chinese people to choose their own political future. Public support will demonstrate to China that the international community is not backing down on human rights, and to prodemocracy activists in Hong Kong and China that they are not alone. A newly-released report by Freedom House on *Supporting Democracy Abroad* found that in U.S. foreign policy toward China "immediate economic and strategic interests almost always override support for democracy and human rights." It is crucial for U.S. policymakers to understand that supporting the people of Hong Kong in their quest for democracy is not only morally right but also pragmatic. A free and democratic Hong Kong is also an economically prosperous Hong Kong, which makes for better business and stronger partnerships. As noted in the U.S.-Hong Kong Policy Act of 1992, "the human rights of the people of Hong Kong are of great importance to the United States and are directly relevant to United States interests in Hong Kong

. . . Human rights also serve as a basis for Hong Kong's continued economic prosperity."[3]

2. Multilateral efforts are important. Democratic nations should work together to express support for the people of Hong Kong while condemning violations of human rights and exhorting China to uphold its handover promises of maintaining the one country, two systems model. If the United States acts alone without a chorus of other democracies, it is subject to the fabricated CCP narrative that the United States is picking on China. It is difficult for China to accuse protesters of doing the bidding of the Central Intelligence Agency if numerous nations are communicating the same message. Specific multilateral initiatives could include:

• Efforts at the United Nations to pass a resolution urging the Hong Kong government to genuinely implement the ICCPR—including provisions on freedom expression and assembly and on elections—and uphold its commitment to human rights;

• A visit to Hong Kong by the UN Special Rapporteur on the Rights to Freedom of Peaceful Assembly and of Association, to assess whether the government of Hong Kong is honoring citizens' rights to freely assemble and associate.

• Resolutions in the legislative bodies of democratic nations expressing support for the right of the citizens of Hong Kong to determine their future;

• Efforts to identify points of economic leverage that would allow the international community to increase pressure on Chinese authorities to follow the law and its past pledges, and respect Hong Kong's special status.

3. Congress can also play a powerful role in supporting democracy and human rights in Hong Kong and China. Though multilateral efforts are important, this does not mean the U.S. and its legislative branch should be soft-spoken. Congress can take several effective actions to highlight and bolster human rights in Hong Kong and China, including:

• Urging the Hong Kong government to uphold its commitments to the ICCPR and listen to its citizens' demands for free and democratic elections.

• Renewing the section 301 reporting requirements found in the United States-Hong Kong Policy Act of 1992, which required the State Department to report to Congress on "conditions of interest to the United States . . . including developments related to the change in the exercise of sovereignty over Hong Kong," and "the development of democratic institutions in Hong Kong." The last of these reports was submitted in 2007, and an updated assessment would assist you as legislators seized with Hong Kong's and China's freer futures. The counterpart bills, S. 2922 and H.R. 5696, do just that, and I commend you, Mr. Chairmen, for the bipartisan and bicameral effort to introduce such legislation.

• Maintaining vigorous Radio Free Asia and Voice of America broadcasting in Cantonese is also important, and I again commend you for recognizing this as a priority in the bicameral legislation you have introduced.

• Tying any U.S. differential (i.e., better) treatment of Hong Kong—vis-à-vis China as a whole—to that region's veritable autonomy. Your legislation's presidential certification to this effect represents a strong policy.

• And, Congress should also send a congressional delegation to Hong Kong to meet with government leaders, observe the protests, and assess any negotiations that occur between protestors and the government authorities.

CONCLUSION

We are at a pivotal moment for democracy in Hong Kong. If there is one thing history has show us, it is this: Authoritarian rule has a limited life span. No matter how hard the CCP may try to quash dissent, outlaw religious belief, control the outcome of so-called elections, manipulate economic prosperity, or control the words and thoughts of its citizens, it is on the wrong side of history. No regime can outlast the inherent appeal of universal values among average citizens, and we must all join in supporting the democratic aspirations of the people of Hong Kong.

At the moment of Hong Kong's 1997 handover of sovereignty from the United Kingdom to China, when I was a House leadership staffer working on the issue, the question could rightly be asked, "Will Hong Kong positively infect the rest of China with its freedoms, or will China negatively infect Hong Kong with its lack of them?" This moment some seventeen years later is a crucial juncture in answering that question. It matters to the future freedom of China as a whole. The Chinese people will be watching. It is no time for the United States and self-respecting democratic nations to be coy and muted.

---

[3] PL102–383

Thank you for the opportunity to testify before you today. I look forward to your questions.

————

PREPARED STATEMENT OF RICHARD C. BUSH

NOVEMBER 20, 2014

Chairman Brown, Chairman Smith, thank you for giving me the privilege to testify today. This is an important issue for U.S. policy and for me personally. I lived in Hong Kong as a teenager and followed the issue during the dozen years I was on the staff of the House Foreign Affairs Committee. In 1992, I played a staff role in the House consideration of the U.S.-Hong Policy Act.

I have four general themes:

Theme Number One: Hong Kong is important to the United States and U.S.-China relations primarily because it is a test of the proposition that ethnic Chinese people are perfectly capable of democratic citizenship. Hong Kong can and should be an example of Chinese government that is representative, accountable, and effective—the sort of government that Americans would like to see emerge in China someday.

Let me stress four words in that last sentence.

- Example: Chinese leaders and their citizens will be more likely to choose democracy, whatever its flaws, when they see that it works well in Chinese societies like Hong Kong and Taiwan.
- Representative: for Hong Kong's system to be representative, the candidates for major elections must offer voters a choice between all major points of view.
- Accountable: elections give citizens the opportunity to confer legitimacy on leaders when they do well and hold them accountable when they do not.
- Effective: The majority of Hong Kong people no doubt want a democratic system for its own sake, but they also expect that it will address the problems in their everyday lives.

There are, of course, other American interests at play in Hong Kong. About 1,200 American companies have a presence there, along with a very active American Chamber of Commerce. Approximately, 60,000 Americans live there. Many more U.S. residents of Hong Kong origin live in the United States, and make a significant contribution to our society. Still, I would rate Hong Kong's political future as the most important U.S. interest.

Theme Number Two: the U.S.-Hong Kong Policy Act remains a sound foundation for American policy.

Its policy prescriptions remain valid, and its emphasis on the preservation of Hong Kong's autonomy in areas that are critical to American interests is more important today than it was twenty-two years ago. I believed in 1992 and believe now that Section 202, regarding suspension of the application of U.S. laws in the event that Hong Kong's autonomy is circumscribed, is the most important provision of the legislation.

Regarding the bill you have introduced, Mr. Chairmen, I support the resumption of the State Department reports on developments in Hong Kong. Actually, I believe that the Administration should resume the reports on its own without waiting for legislation, because that would be a good and timely signal. Whoever initiates the resumption of the report, it is important as there be a serious Congressional commitment to hold regular hearings on Hong Kong and U.S. policy.

I am agnostic on your proposal to require the President to certify that Hong Kong is sufficiently autonomous before any new laws, agreements and arrangements are applied to it. Implicit in the original law's requirement that the President make judgments about the applicability of *existing* laws, agreements, and arrangements is the idea that the President make the same sort of judgment about *new* ones. As useful as certification might be, substantive consultations between the two branches on this matter would be just as important.

Theme Number Three: what has happened in Hong Kong over the last three months was not foreordained. The protest movement was the product of a series of choices by the parties involved, particularly the government of China. Here I would make the following sub-points.

First of all, when Beijing enacted the Basic Law for Hong Kong in 1990, it created a political system that provided extraordinary power and influence to some social groups over others. The Hong Kong business community was particularly privileged and the middle class was disadvantaged.

Second, as a result, the middle class came to recognize that public protest was the only mode of political participation open to it. And in some cases, protests actually worked to secure the withdrawal of policy initiatives that lacked public support.

Third, in my view, back in the spring and summer of this year there was available a compromise on how to elect Hong Kong's chief executive. The approach I have in mind would have ensured that the candidates running for chief executive would likely have offered voters a choice among the range of public views on government policy. Such an approach would likely have received support from at least some in the democratic camp and therefore could have secured Legislative Council approval.

As an aside, I should say that Beijing's choice to allow elections on a one-person-one-vote basis is an improvement over the existing arrangement of having an unrepresentative, 1,200-person committee to pick the chief executive.

The problem, of course, is China's method for picking the candidates, and the fear of many in Hong Kong that Beijing in effect would screen candidates. The compromise that I believe was available would have liberalized the composition and processes of the nominating committee. It would have been consistent with the Basic Law (a Chinese requirement) and likely ensured a competitive election. There were Hong Kong proposals along these lines, but the decision of the PRC National People's Congress Standing Committee on August 31st ignored them. That decision was unacceptable to a majority of Hong Kong people because it did not *guarantee* a competitive election in which a range of policy approaches was at play.

Fourth, the protest movement was assuredly about ensuring genuinely competitive elections and representative government, but it was also fueled by widespread public dissatisfaction over inequality of income, wealth, opportunities for good jobs, and access to affordable housing. A democratic system is seen as the solution to these problems. But even if a truly democratic system is established, if that system fails to address these problems, confidence in democracy will wane.

Fifth, the protest movement has had a number of deficiencies. It is divided among different social and generational groups, all competing for initiative. It became fixated on one means of ensuring a competitive election—civic nomination—and not on the goal itself. It has lacked a clear strategy and unity of command, which in turn has made it very difficult for it to define success and then engineer a negotiated end to the crisis.

And an end to the crisis is needed. The citizens who initially supported the protests and those that did not are increasingly unhappy about the disruption that that they must cope with every day. Some older leaders of the movement are calling on their younger comrades to end the occupation of major thoroughfares. No one should assume that the occupation can continue forever or that will Beijing will ultimately back down. The opportunity to avoid a coercive or violent crackdown—and to avoid new constraints on Hong Kong's civil and political liberties—should be seized and seized soon.

Sixth, there is reason to believe that even within the parameters laid down by Beijing on August 31st, it still remains possible to engineer a nominating process that has a competitive character. Senior Hong Kong officials have hinted as much.

Theme Number Four: the United States Government has pursued a skillful threading of the policy needle, and it should continue to do so.

The Administration has been measured, clear, balanced, and pointed in its rhetorical statements on the current situation. I would refer you in particular to the White House statement of September 29th. The Administration has signaled its support for a genuinely democratic solution. It recognizes that if Hong Kong people can, with Beijing's concurrence, work out a mutually acceptable solution to the challenge of constitutional reform, it will be more enduring because they were the ones that achieved it.

I will say that Washington is constrained somewhat by the reflexive tendency of the Chinese government to blame whatever trouble it is facing on outsiders, instead of recognizing its own policy failures. In the Hong Kong case, Beijing and its propaganda organs have put out the canard that the U.S. government is the "black hand" behind the current protest movement. Nothing could be further from the truth, of course, and Beijing has had to grasp at straws to make its case. I am pleased that last week in Beijing, President Obama authoritatively made clear to President Xi Jinping that the Hong Kong protest movement was home grown. Taking Beijing's misperceptions into account is necessary because of the actions that it may take based on those misperceptions. But having taken that factor into account, the U.S. government should not refrain from doing what it believes is needed to protect and promote our interests.

Let me assure you, by the way, that our diplomats in Hong Kong are skilled professionals who understand both the promise and the problems of the current situa-

tion. Among other things, they understand what all of us should appreciate: the need to hear a range of Hong Kong views. And a range does exist. There are sensible people in both the establishment and democratic camp, people who understand the need to address all of Hong Kong's governance problems through a political system that is representative, accountable, and effective. We should take our cues from people in Hong Kong who have an accurate appreciation of its problems and good judgment about how to solve them.

———

PREPARED STATEMENT OF HON. SHERROD BROWN, A U.S. SENATOR FROM OHIO; CHAIRMAN, CONGRESSIONAL-EXECUTIVE COMMISSION ON CHINA

NOVEMBER 20, 2014

Thank you all for attending this important hearing on the future of democracy in Hong Kong.

There is bipartisan concern in the U.S. over the future of Hong Kong, as you can tell by my colleagues who have joined me on the dais today.

For the first time in this organization's history, the two chairs of this Commission have led a bipartisan effort to introduce legislation, in this case to renew our commitment to freedom and democracy in Hong Kong.

I commend my co-chair, Congressman Chris Smith, for working with me on this issue.

I also thank our Republican and Democratic co-sponsors, some of whom have joined us today.

The legislation, called the *Hong Kong Human Rights and Democracy Act,* is a much-needed amendment to the 1992 Hong Kong Policy Act. It reinstitutes reporting requirements that lapsed in 2007 and requires the President to certify that Hong Kong remains sufficiently autonomous before undertaking any new laws or agreements that treat Hong Kong different from China.

We urge quick passage of this bipartisan bill.

Why are we in Washington so concerned about Hong Kong?

China made a promise. China made a promise to the international community and to the people of Hong Kong that they could enjoy certain freedoms and freely elect their leaders. It is those freedoms and autonomy that have ensured Hong Kong's stability and prosperity.

But now China is backtracking on these promises and threatening the future viability of Hong Kong as an international finance center and a free city.

Not only that, Chinese leaders are seeking to distract from the issue by claiming that the protests are part of some foreign conspiracy, masterminded by the United States.

Nothing could be further from the truth.

As we have all witnessed, the students, the workers, and the ordinary citizens who have demonstrated at great risk to their livelihood represent a genuine desire.

It is a universal wish for basic freedoms and democracy.

It is a wish that no amount of money can replace.

Hong Kong is a test of China's willingness to comply with its international commitments.

If China can so easily renege on its promises to Hong Kong, then how can we expect China to hold up its end of the bargain on issues like World Trade Organization compliance or future trade agreements?

As the democracy movement in Hong Kong enters a new phase, we call on the Hong Kong government to exercise restraint, engage in genuine dialogue with the protesters, and to respect their peaceful calls for democracy.

We call on China to fulfill the commitment it made to allow the people of Hong Kong to run and vote in free and fair elections.

We also send a message to the people of Hong Kong and China, that they have an ally in the United States.

We will continue to monitor the situation closely and to speak out whenever the universal freedoms of the people of Hong Kong and China are threatened.

I look forward to the testimony of the esteemed witnesses.

37

PREPARED STATEMENT OF HON. CHRISTOPHER SMITH, A U.S. REPRESENTATIVE FROM NEW JERSEY; COCHAIRMAN, CONGRESSIONAL-EXECUTIVE COMMISSION ON CHINA

NOVEMBER 20, 2014

Thank you, Chairman Brown, for calling this hearing. I would like to welcome our witnesses and thank them for agreeing to testify today. The future of Hong Kong's democracy is truly an international concern as the presence of Lord Patten and the other witnesses here today confirms. I look forward to your testimony.

This is the second public event that the Commission has held on the issue of Hong Kong. In April, the Commission heard from Martin Lee and Anson Chan, two veterans of Hong Kong's political world. There work, as well as the work of Hong Kong's new generation of leaders, has inspired this Commission and the U.S. Congress.

As has been mentioned already, Senator Brown and I have introduced bills in the House and Senate to update U.S. policy on Hong Kong. I have also agreed to start the Congressional Hong Kong Caucus, to demonstrate the Congress's concern about Hong Kong's autonomy and its importance to U.S. national interests.

As our witnesses today will attest, under the "one country, two systems" model, China guaranteed that Hong Kong could retain its separate political, legal, and economic systems for at least 50 years. Hong Kong's constitution, the Basic Law, protects the rights of the people of Hong Kong to free speech, assembly, and the power to choose their own government, ultimately through universal suffrage.

These promises were made to the people of Hong Kong and to the international community.

Instead of keeping these promises, Beijing has decided to stack the desk against democracy and the rule of law, demanding that both judges and any future Chief Executive must "love the country and love Hong Kong." In August of this year, Beijing further ruled the people of Hong Kong could not freely choose their next leader.

Such demands will undermine an independent judiciary and make the 2017 Chief Executive election look more like an Iranian election than one that is free and fair.

The slow erosion of press freedoms and the rule of law, the setbacks to Hong Kong's democratic developments, and Beijing's less than subtle oversight of Hong Kong are the reasons the protests materialized and why they are ongoing. No matter what is said by President Xi or other Chinese officials, the "Umbrella Movement" was a creation of Beijing's policies and its rough oversight.

There is no "black hand" of foreign forces behind the protests, only requests for Beijing to live up to its promises and to ensure Hong Kong's unique system of autonomy within China.

Hong Kong's unique system has ensured prosperity and spurred the type of creativity that only comes with the advance of fundamental freedoms. The freedoms of speech, assembly, association, and religion, and an independent judiciary, are the foundation on which Hong Kong's continued prosperity and stability are based.

This is what the people of Hong Kong want, it is what they have conveyed to their leaders, and to Beijing repeatedly for the past 17 years.

Hong Kong's continued autonomy and the advance of its democracy is a concern of the U.S. Congress and of freedom-loving peoples everywhere.

If given a real choice, people everywhere vote to advance representative governments that protect the rule of law and the fundamental freedoms of speech, assembly, association, and religion. The people of Mainland China do not have such a choice and attempts to pursue universally-recognized rights are often met with repression and harassment.

This cannot be Hong Kong's future.

Hong Kong is the true embodiment of the "China Dream" and that fact may scare some in the Communist Party. We stand with those who want Hong Kong to remain free, vital, prosperous, and democratic—as Beijing has long promised.

www.ingramcontent.com/pod-product-compliance
Lightning Source LLC
Chambersburg PA
CBHW080930290526
45795CB00007BA/2694

(II)

THE FUTURE OF DEMOCRACY IN HONG KONG

HEARING

BEFORE THE

CONGRESSIONAL-EXECUTIVE COMMISSION ON CHINA

ONE HUNDRED THIRTEENTH CONGRESS

SECOND SESSION

NOVEMBER 20, 2014

Printed for the use of the Congressional-Executive Commission on China

Available via the World Wide Web: http://www.cecc.gov

U.S. GOVERNMENT PUBLISHING OFFICE

92–631 PDF   WASHINGTON : 2015

For sale by the Superintendent of Documents, U.S. Government Publishing Office
Internet: bookstore.gpo.gov   Phone: toll free (866) 512–1800; DC area (202) 512–1800
Fax: (202) 512–2104   Mail: Stop IDCC, Washington, DC 20402–0001